12/18

D

BRAIDING HAIR

By Dana Meachen Rau • Illustrated by Kathleen Petelinsek

CHERRY LAKE PUBLISHING • ANN ARBOR, MICHIGAN

CHERRY LAKE Publishing

Published in the United States of America by Cherry Lake Publishing
Ann Arbor, Michigan
www.cherrylakepublishing.com

Content Adviser: Dr. Julia L. Hovanec, Professor of Art Education,
Kutztown University, Kutztown, Pennsylvania

Photo Credits: Pages 4 and 5, ©CREATISTA/Shutterstock, Inc.; page
6, ©Subbotina Anna/Shutterstock, Inc.; page 8, ©urosr/Shutterstock,
Inc.; page 9, ©Jacek Kadaj/Shutterstock, Inc.; pages 20, 26, 28, and
30, ©Dana Meachen Rau; page 29, ©Maria Dryfhout/Shutterstock, Inc.;
page 32, ©Tania McNaboe

Library of Congress Cataloging-in-Publication Data
Rau, Dana Meachen, 1971–
  Braiding hair / by Dana Meachen Rau.
    p. cm. — (How-to library. Crafts)
  Audience: Grade 4 to 6
  Includes bibliographical references and index.
  ISBN 978-1-61080-471-4 (lib. bdg.) —
ISBN 978-1-61080-558-2 (e-book) — ISBN 978-1-61080-645-9 (pbk.)
1. Braids (Hairdressing)—Juvenile literature. I. Title.
  TT975.R38 2012
  646.7'247—dc23   2012009658

Cherry Lake Publishing would like to acknowledge the work
of The Partnership for 21st Century Skills. Please visit
www.21stcenturyskills.org for more information.

Printed in the United States of America
Corporate Graphics Inc.
July 2012
CLFA11

A NOTE TO ADULTS:
Please review the instructions for these craft projects before your children make them. Be sure to help them with any crafts you do not think they can safely conduct on their own.

A NOTE TO KIDS:
Be sure to ask an adult for help with these craft activities when you need it. Always put your safety first!

HOW-TO LIBRARY

TABLE OF CONTENTS

Unique Hairdos

Braiding can be a social event with friends.

Everyone is unique. Close your eyes and think of your friends and family. What makes each of them different and special? One thing you might think of is their hair. It may be blond, brown, red, black, white, or gray. It might be short or long. It could be straight, wavy, or curly. It could be thin or thick.

Do you like to wear your hair down? Or do you prefer pulling it up into a ponytail or pushing it back with a headband?

Braiding is a fun way to weave your hair into interesting designs. Braids are like art on your head!

You can braid your own hair. Braiding can also be a social event. Practice on a friend, and let your friend practice on you. Learn how to do basic braids. Then try the styles in this book. Don't be afraid to experiment with your own ideas to create a unique braided hairdo of your own!

ALL KINDS OF HAIR
The type of hair you have often depends on your **ethnic** group and the traits passed down by your parents. You might have very straight, dark hair or very tight curly spirals of hair. You may have long, thin, blond hair or thick, red hair. Try braids on all types of hair to see how each hairstyle works for different people.

Your hair is as unique as you are!

What Is Hair?

Your hair and fingernails are made of the same stuff.

Hair is made of a substance called **keratin**. This is the same material that makes up your fingernails.

Hair grows out of the skin. The part of the hair under the surface is alive. Each hair sits in a little hole called a **follicle**. Follicles also have **glands** that help coat your hair with oil.

The hair above the surface of the scalp is called the **shaft**. This part of the hair is not alive. That's why it doesn't hurt when you cut it.

Each shaft of hair has a layer of armor called a **cuticle** to protect it. If your hair is too dry, the cuticle can break and your hair can look dull.

Hair gets its coloring from a substance called **melanin**. Hair with more melanin is dark, and hair with less melanin is light.

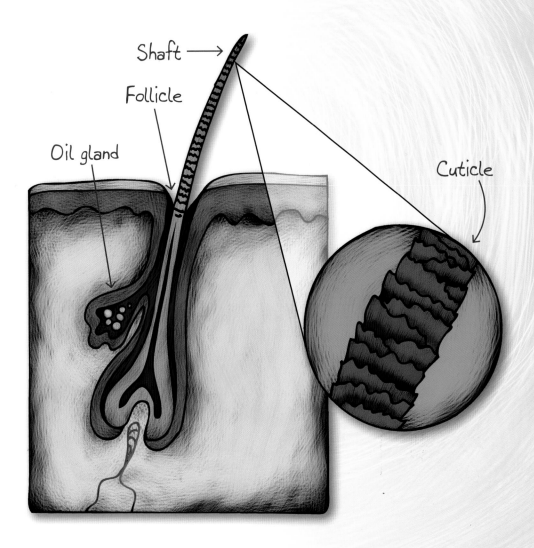

Shaft ⟶

Follicle

Oil gland

Cuticle

Hair in History

Braids and decorated hair have been an important part of some cultures.

Braided hair has played a part in the history of many different cultures around the globe. In Africa, people braided patterns and designs into their hair. The Viking women of northern Europe had long, blond braids. Native American men and women decorated their braids with feathers, shells, and beads.

Braided hair had a practical purpose. It was a good way to keep hair neat and pulled away from the face while people worked. But people also braided their hair for other reasons. Fancier braided styles could express a person's importance. Certain braided patterns were saved for important events or celebrations. Braiding was also a way for people to spend time with each other.

You can express your personality with braids. What will your braid say about you?

Braiding styles can be different in different places.

Three-Strand Basic Braiding

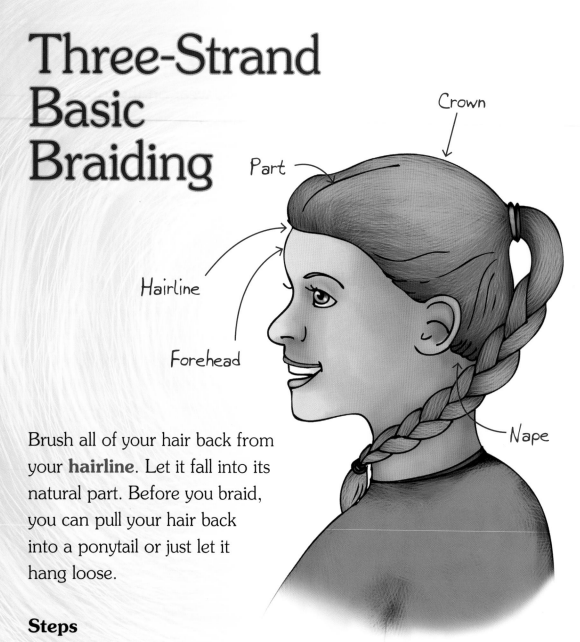

Crown

Part

Hairline

Forehead

Nape

Brush all of your hair back from your **hairline**. Let it fall into its natural part. Before you braid, you can pull your hair back into a ponytail or just let it hang loose.

Steps

1. Divide the hair into three equal strands.
2. Hold the left strand in your left hand. Hold the right strand in your right hand. Cross the right strand over the middle strand. Hold the new middle strand in place with your right thumb.

3. Cross the left strand over the middle strand. Hold the new middle strand in place with your left thumb.

4. Continue crossing the right strand and then the left strand over the middle strand. As you work, keep the strands secure, but don't pull too tight. Slide your hand down the strands once in a while to smooth them out.

5. When you reach the end of the braid, secure with a hair elastic.

Continue crossing over the strands until you reach the end.

Hand position can be tricky. It will also be different depending on whether you are braiding a friend's hair or your own. Practice to find the way that works best for you. If you don't have a friend nearby to practice on, you may have a doll with hair you can braid. She won't complain if you tug too hard by mistake!

Two-Strand Fishtail Braiding

This type of braid is also called a herringbone braid.

To start a fishtail braid, brush all of your hair back from your hairline. Like the three-strand basic braid, you can pull your hair into a ponytail, or you can let it hang loose and start the braid at the **nape** of the neck.

Steps

1. Divide the hair into two equal strands. Hold one in each hand with your palms facing up.

Start with two strands.

2. With your left index finger, divide a thin section of hair from the outside of the left strand. Reach over with your right hand and cross this section over to the inside of the right strand.

3. With your right index finger, divide a thin section from the outside of the right strand. Reach over with your left hand and cross this section over to the inside of the left strand.

4. Continue all the way down the braid, **alternating** left and right. Try to keep the new added strands of hair the same size. Then your braid will look more uniform.

5. When you reach the end of the braid, secure it with a hair elastic.

Keep adding thin sections of hair to the opposite strand.

ELASTIC TIP
Make sure you have your hair elastic handy before you start braiding. You can keep it on your wrist. Then it's right there when you need it.

French Braiding

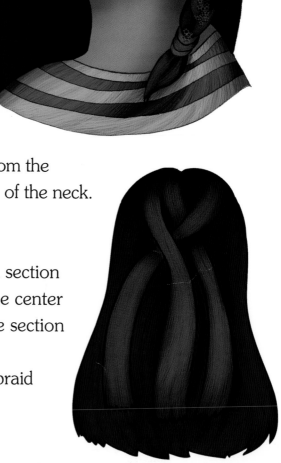

You can adapt French braid skills to many unique hairdos.

To make this French braid, you will pick up new sections of hair as you braid from the crown of the head to the nape of the neck.

Steps

1. Use a tail comb to make a section of hair at the hairline in the center of the forehead. Divide the section of hair into three strands.
2. Start a three-strand basic braid (*see pages 12–13*).

3. Cross over the right strand and hold it in place with your left thumb. With your right hand, pick up a small section of hair from the hairline toward your braid. You can also use a tail comb to help you pick up a new section of hair. Add this new section to the crossed-over strand.

VARIATIONS ON THE FRENCH BRAID

Once you've mastered the French braid, try dividing the hair into two sections with a part down the middle for "pigtail" French braids. Or use a section of hair parted from one ear to the other to make a braided "headband."

If you cross the strands under each other instead of over as you braid, you will create a braid that sits on top of the hair. This overbraiding technique is used to make cornrows—tiny braids made with small sections of hair that are braided close to the scalp.

4. Cross over the left strand and hold it in place with your right thumb. Pick up a small section of hair on the left side. Add it to the crossed-over strand.

5. Continue working from the crown to the nape, adding sections of hair on each side. Keep braiding even after you've run out of extra hair to pick up.

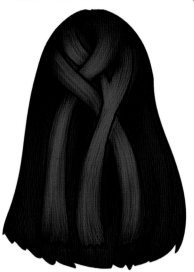

Continue a basic braid to the end once you reach the nape.

Braided Rose Bun

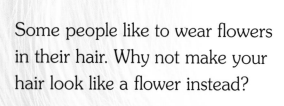

This style works well for keeping hair off your face for dance classes.

Some people like to wear flowers in their hair. Why not make your hair look like a flower instead?

Materials
Brush
2 hair elastics
1½-inch-wide (3.8 centimeters wide) green ribbon, about 12 to 15 inches (30 to 38 cm) long
Scissors
Bobby pins

Steps

1. Brush the hair back from the hairline. Gather it together into a high ponytail and secure it with a hair elastic.

2. Separate the ponytail hair into three strands. Braid a three-strand basic braid (*see pages 12–13*). Secure the end of the braid with the other hair elastic.
3. Tie the ribbon around the base of the braid in a double overhand knot (not a bow), so the ends stick out on each side.
4. Cut the ribbon ends to a point so they look like leaves.
5. Wrap the braid around its base. Try to cover the ribbon and knot so that all you see are the two "leaves" sticking out the sides.
6. Continue wrapping the braid around the base until you run out of hair. Secure the end with a bobby pin pushed into the base of the bun.
7. **Reinforce** the rest of the bun with bobby pins by sticking them around the bottom of the bun from the outside into the center.

Stick pins into the bun from all sides.

BOUQUET OF ROSES
Make two, three, four, or more ponytails on your head. Coil each one into a rose bun to make a head full of "flowers."

Hidden Fairy Braids

Just like fairies like to hide in the forest, you can weave little hidden braids into your hair. They'll peek out from under your flowing hair.

Jazz up your fairy braids with beads.

Materials

Tail comb
2 holding clips
10 lengths of
$\frac{1}{8}$-inch-wide (0.3 cm) satin ribbon, each about 2 to 3 inches (5 to 8 cm) longer than your hair
30 plastic pony beads
10 hair elastics

Steps

1. With a tail comb, make a part around the crown of the head. Hold this hair up and out of the way with a holding clip.
2. Starting at the part, gather a small section of hair about 1 inch (2.5 cm) wide. Tie a piece of ribbon to the top of the section in a small knot.

3. Divide the section of hair into two strands. Braid a three-strand basic braid using the two hair strands and one ribbon piece (*see pages 12–13*). Secure the end temporarily with another holding clip.

4. Thread 3 beads onto the end of the braid (*see instructions on page 30*). Secure the end of the braid with a hair elastic.

5. Repeat steps 2 to 4 nine more times around the head at the part.

6. When you are done, unclip the hair from the crown. Let if flow over the braids.

Use a ribbon as one of the three strands.

When you are done, let the crown hair fall back over the braids.

Glitter Crown

Treat yourself like royalty. Turn a basic braid into a jeweled crown by weaving in metallic ribbon and dotting your hairdo with gems.

Materials

Tail comb

6 hair elastics

Metallic rickrack

Bobby pins

Gem bobby pins

   (*see instructions on
the next page*)

*Turn two simple
braids into a fancy
headpiece.*

Steps

1. With a tail comb, make a part down the center of the head. Pull the hair on each side into ponytails behind the ears.

2. Divide each ponytail into three strands. Braid each ponytail into a three-strand basic braid (*see pages 12–13*). Secure the ends with hair elastics.

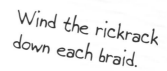
Wind the rickrack down each braid.

3. Cut one length of rickrack about the same length as the braid. Tie the rickrack to the base of the braid with an overhand knot.

4. Wind the rickrack around and around the braid from base to end. When you reach the end, secure it with another hair elastic over the first one. Repeat steps 3 and 4 on the other braid.

5. Cross one of the braids over the top of the head. Use a bobby pin to secure the end of the braid to the top of the hair.

6. Cross the other braid over the top of the head and pin the end in place. Add a few more bobby pins along the braids to secure them to the hair.

7. Decorate the braids with gem bobby pins.

HOW TO MAKE GEM BOBBY PINS
Buy a variety of plastic gems at a craft store. Use strong glue to attach them to the ends of bobby pins. Let them dry completely before wearing. You wouldn't want your hair to get caught in the glue!

Wavy Seashore Braid

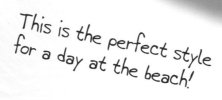

Make waves with this fishtail braid. Complete the theme by wrapping the end in rope and adding some seashell barrettes.

This is the perfect style for a day at the beach!

Materials
Brush
Tail comb
1 small hair elastic
12-inch (30-cm) length of thin rope
Scissors
2 shell barrettes

Steps
1. Brush the hair back from the hairline. Use the pointy end of a tail comb to divide the hair into two sections.

2. Braid a two-strand fishtail braid (*see pages 14–15*).
   Secure the end with a small hair elastic.

3. To wrap the end with rope, bend one end
   of the rope so you have about a 3-inch
   (7.5 cm) tail. Hold the looped part of the
   rope against the end of the braid.

4. Starting slightly below the elastic, wrap the
   longer tail of the rope around and around
   the bottom of the braid, toward the nape
   of the neck. Cover the elastic and continue
   up a few more coils. Make sure the coils lay
   neatly next to, not on top of, each other.
   Make sure the loop is still visible at the top.

5. Thread the long end of the rope through
   the loop at the top. Carefully pull on the
   bottom and top ends of the rope to make a knot under
   the coils. Snip off the ends of the rope with scissors.

6. Clip the two shell barrettes (*see instructions below*)
   on either side of your head to hold up any loose hairs.

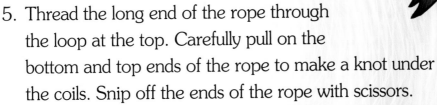

HOW TO MAKE SHELL
BARRETTES
Collect small seashells or buy
some at a craft store. Attach
them to hair barrettes with strong
glue. Be sure to let them dry
completely before wearing them.

Tropical Paradise Braids

When the sun burns hot, you need to keep cool. With this exotic hairstyle, you can look cool, too! Three French braids joined together with a bouquet of silk flowers creates a tropical vacation look.

You can add ribbons and feathers to your flowery elastic.

Materials
Brush
Tail comb
2 holding clips
3 small hair elastics
1 large hair elastic
Colorful silk flowers

Work across the head from left to right.

Steps

1. With a tail comb, divide the hair into three equal sections by making one part over the crown of the head from ear to ear and the another part across the back of the head. Keep the front and back sections separate with holding clips.

2. Starting with the middle section, French braid from the hairline on the left side of the head to the right (*see pages 16–17*). Continue even after you no longer have hair to pick up. Secure the end of the braid with a small hair elastic.

3. Repeat step 2 on the front section. If you have bangs, you can include them in this section. Or you can let them hang on your forehead and just pick up a section of hair behind them.

4. Repeat step 2 on the back section. You will now have three French braids.

5. Gather the ends of the three braids together with the larger hair elastic.

6. If your silk flowers have small stems, simply tuck them into the elastic. If not, sew them onto a hair elastic (*see instructions below*) and use it to secure the three braids together.

Join all three braids with one elastic.

HOW TO MAKE FLOWER ELASTICS

Thread a sewing needle and knot the end of the thread. Stitch back and forth about five times into the flower and around the elastic. Tie a knot and clip the extra thread with scissors.

Benefits of Braiding

Braiding isn't just a way to wear your hair. It has many other benefits. If you play sports, it's a good way to keep your hair out of your face. It also keeps hair off your neck to keep you cool on a hot day. Depending on the type of hair you have, you may be able to keep your braids in for more than one day.

Braids can also reflect your personality. Two braids with bows might show people you are playful. A fancy bun or crown braid says that you are **sophisticated**. Make your own style to show off how you see the world.

Braiding also brings people together. Find a friend and learn how to braid as a team. Get help from a parent, aunt, uncle, or grandparent. Spend time learning, chatting, and braiding together.

HEALTHY HAIR
Hair needs healthy nutrients to grow. Nutrients are in the food you eat. If you eat healthy food, your hair will get the food it needs, too.

Braids keep your hair out of your eyes so you can concentrate on playing.

Glossary

alternating (AWL-tur-nay-ting) going back and forth between two things

crown (KROUN) the top part of the head

cuticle (KYOO-ti-kuhl) the outer layer of a shaft of hair

ethnic (ETH-nik) having to do with a group of people sharing the same national origins, language, or culture

follicle (FAH-li-kuhl) a small hole in your skin where hair grows

glands (GLANDZ) body organs that produce or release natural chemicals

hairline (HAIR-line) where the hair meets your face at the forehead

keratin (KER-uh-tin) the substance hair is made of

melanin (MEL-uh-nin) the substance that gives hair color

nape (NAPE) the back of the neck

reinforce (ree-in-FORS) make stronger or more secure

shaft (SHAFT) the part of your hair above the surface of your skin

sophisticated (suh-FIS-tuh-kay-tid) having a lot of knowledge about culture and fashion

Adding Beads

1. Bend a pipe cleaner in half. Twist the ends together to make a loop at one end so it looks like an oversized sewing needle.
2. Thread the beads onto the pointy end.
3. Stick the end of the braid through the loop.
4. Push the beads up the needle, over the looped end, and onto the braid.
5. Secure the end of the braid with a hair elastic. Be sure to use one large enough to keep the beads from falling off your braid.

For More Information

Books

Jones, Jen. *Braiding Hair: Beyond the Basics*. Mankato, MN: Capstone Press, 2009.

Jordan, Jim. *Hair: Styling Tips and Tricks for Girls*. Middleton, WI: American Girl, 2000.

Krull, Kathleen. *Big Wig: A Little History of Hair*. New York: Arthur A. Levine Books, 2011.

Neuman, Maria. *Fabulous Hair*. New York: DK Publishing, 2006.

Swain, Ruth Freeman. *Hairdo! What We Do and Did to Our Hair*. New York: Holiday House, 2002.

Web Sites

Discovery Kids: Human Hair

http://yucky.discovery.com/flash/body/pg000148.html

Find out more about why people have different types of hair.

KidsHealth: Your Hair

http://kidshealth.org/kid/cancer_center/HTBW/hair.html

Learn more about how your body grows hair and how to keep your hair healthy.

Princess Hairstyles

www.princesshairstyles.com

Check out some fun new braiding styles.

Index

About the Author

Dana Meachen Rau is the author of more than 300 books for children on many topics, including science, history, cooking, and crafts. She creates, experiments, researches, and writes from her home office in Burlington, Connecticut.